D1088256

A Short History of
HALLOWEEN

by **Sally Lee**

Consulting Editor: Gail Saunders-Smith, PhD
Consultant: Jeannine Diddle Uzzi, PhD,
Director of Faculty Programs,
Associated Colleges of the South

CAPSTONE PRESS
a capstone imprint

Pebble Plus is published by Capstone Press,
1710 Roe Crest Drive, North Mankato, Minnesota 56003
www.capstonepub.com

Library of Congress Cataloging-in-Publication Data
Lee, Sally.
  A short history of Halloween / by Sally Lee.
      pages cm.—(Pebble plus. Holiday histories)
  Includes bibliographical references and index.
  ISBN 978-1-4914-6096-2 (library binding)—ISBN 978-1-4914-6100-6 (pbk.)—ISBN 978-1-4914-6104-4 (ebook pdf)
  1. Halloween—Juvenile literature. I. Title.
  GT4965.L355 2016
  394.2646—dc23   2015002028

Editorial Credits
Erika L. Shores, editor; Bobbie Nuytten, designer; Kelly Garvin, media researcher;
Lori Barbeau, production specialist

Photo Credits
Art Resource/Scala, 11; Capstone Press/Karon Dubke, 15; Corbis: Historical Picture Archive, 13, Stapleton Collection, 7; Getty Images/Hulton Archive, 9; iStockphoto/mediaphotos, 21; Shutterstock: Cattallina, cover (cobweb), Daniel Schweinert, 19, Honza Krej, cover, James Steidl, 17, Lisa Alisa, cover (bats), SeanLockePhotography, 5, surassawadee, cover (tree)

Design elements: Shutterstock: Aohodesign, Gokce Gurellier

Note to Parents and Teachers

The Holiday Histories set supports national curriculum standards for social studies. This book describes and illustrates the holiday of Halloween. The images support early readers in understanding the text. The repetition of words and phrases helps early readers learn new words. This book also introduces early readers to subject-specific vocabulary words, which are defined in the Glossary section. Early readers may need assistance to read some words and to use the Table of Contents, Glossary, Read More, Internet Sites, Critical Thinking Using the Common Core, and Index sections of the book.

Printed in the United States of America in North Mankato, Minnesota.
042015   008823CGF15

Table of Contents

A Spooky Holiday

Today is October 31.

It is Halloween. We see

costumes, candy, and pumpkins.

Let's learn the story behind

this spooky holiday.

Long ago people called
the Celts held a festival
around November 1. It was
called Samhain. Celts thought
spirits visited them on Samhain.

Say Celt: KELT
Say Samhain: SOW-ehn

Samhain also celebrated the end of summer and fall harvest. People had fires, ate large meals, and danced.

All Hallows' Eve

In the 800s Christian leaders
made November 1 All Saints' Day.
Some called it All Hallows' Day.
All Hallows' Eve was the night
before. We now call it Halloween.

All Souls' Day

November 2 became All Souls' Day.

It honored people who had died.

Poor people went to houses asking

for soul cakes. They prayed for

the family's dead loved ones.

13

Trick-or-Treat

The Celts wore masks and costumes to scare away spirits. Kids dress up to trick-or-treat today. They go as animals, ghosts, or movie characters.

Halloween Symbols

Many objects we see at Halloween come from Samhain. Ghosts and skeletons stand for death. Corn, pumpkins, and scarecrows are fall harvest symbols.

A story from Ireland tells

of a ghost named Stingy Jack.

He carried a carved turnip lantern.

Today we carve pumpkins.

We call them jack-o-lanterns.

A Day of Fun

Halloween is a time for parties

and trick-or-treating.

Jack-o-lanterns make

the day spooky. But mostly

Halloween is a lot of fun.

Glossary

Celts—people who lived in Britain and parts of Europe about 2,000 years ago

Christian—having to do with people who follow the teachings of Jesus Christ

festival—a celebration that is held at the same time each year

harvest—to gather crops that are ripe and ready to pick

lantern—a case that light can shine through that can be carried by a handle

saint—a person honored by the Christian church as having lived a very holy life

Samhain—an ancient Celtic festival that marked the end of summer

soul cake—a square of bread with spices and fruits

spirit—the soul or invisible part of a person that is believed to control thoughts and feelings

symbol—a picture or object that stands for something else

trick-or-treating—to go door-to-door asking for candy; this custom comes from the tradition of begging for soul cakes on All Souls' Day

Read More

Felix, Rebecca. *We Celebrate Halloween in Fall.* Let's Look at Fall. Ann Arbor, Mich.: Cherry Lake Pub., 2013.

Heinricks, Ann. *Halloween.* Holidays and Celebrations. North Mankato, Minn.: The Child's World, 2014.

McGee, Randel. *Paper Crafts for Halloween.* Paper Craft Fun for Holidays. Berkeley Heights, N.J.: Enslow, 2013.

Internet Sites

FactHound offers a safe, fun way to find Internet sites related to this book. All of the sites on FactHound have been researched by our staff.

Here's all you do:

Visit *www.facthound.com*

Type in this code: 9781491460962

Check out projects, games and lots more at
www.capstonekids.com

Critical Thinking
Using the Common Core

1. Name some of the symbols that stand for Halloween. (Key Ideas and Details)

2. Explain where our tradition of trick-or-treating comes from. (Integration of Knowledge and Ideas)

Index

Word Count: 213
Grade: 1
Early-Intervention Level: 17